A Penguin's World

PATRICIA GLEICHAUF

Illustrated by Karen Staszko

A Penguin's World

Copyright © 2022 Patricia Gleichauf
Second Edition

Published by Legacy Key Press

All rights reserved

No part of this publication my be reproduced, distributed, or transmitted in any form or by any means,including photocopying, recording,or other electronic or mechanical methods, without the prior written permission of the publisher, except in the case of brief quotations embodied in reviews and certain other noncommercial uses permitted by copyright law.

The moral right of the author has been asserted

Originally published by Page Publishing 2022

ISBN 979-8-9911726-3-9 (soft cover)
ISBN 979-8—9911726-2-2 (hard cover)
ISBN 979-8-9911726-4-6 (digital)

Library of Congress Control Number: 2024915065

Printed in the United States of America

**To Therese and George Anthony for
teaching us how to be good people.
And to Alex, your youngest grandchild. Please watch over him.**

Penguins are the only bird that can swim, but cannot fly through the air. But they can move in more ways than any other bird to get from here to there.

They can paddle, flipper, jump, run, hop,
leap, toboggan, surf, waddle, and slide.
Tobogganing is a great way for penguins to move.
They just flop on their bellies and glide.

Thousands of penguins live in colonies together.
They huddle closely in the coldest weather.
Rotating places gives each some time in the middle of the troop.
The center is the best place to absorb warmth from the group.

Flying birds have bones that are hollow and light. Thin bones have less weight, which helps them with flight.

Penguin bones are solid and stronger.
Heavier bones allow them to swim deeper and longer.

Snares

Oxygen is stored in their bodies allowing penguins to swim underwater for a long while. Their large feet steer them, and their flippers push them faster mile after mile.

When diving for food, penguins are constantly swallowing slippery prey.
Spiny barbs inside of their mouths keep their food from slipping away.

Swimming is what penguins do best.
They must be speedy during a chase.
They leap out of the water like dolphins.
This is called porpoising and helps
them to pick up their pace.

Erect-crested

Penguins flee from predators like seals, birds, snakes, and the fox. They fly through the water, jumping out to hide among the coastal rocks.

Most penguins are black and white.
Only one type has a different hue.
Little fairy penguins are white and blue.

When swimming, penguins' tuxedo colors keep them safer. While their black backs are harder to see by birds flying overhead, their white bellies are hidden from predators lurking in weed beds.

Chinstrap

Only seven types live in the icy water of the Antarctic Ocean. Warmer water nearer the equator is home to the rest. All penguins live in saltwater, choosing the place for their type that is best.

Penguins all make different sounds.
They honk, trumpet, buzz, whistle, quack, growl, or bark like hounds.
Each has a special tone that can be quite loud.
Their unique voice is used to find their family in a crowd.

Magellanic

Their feet are positioned far back in their stance to keep penguins from falling facedown. Stiff tail feathers also help them to stand upright and not tip back to the ground.

Penguins have more feathers than any other bird.
They overlap to cover every inch of their skin.
The thick feathers cushion them in rough seas
and keep cold water from seeping in.

African

In order for their feathers to keep them dry,
they must be kept trimmed and clean.
Penguins routinely pick debris off of their feathers.
It is important for them to preen.

**Penguins only come on land for breeding and molting
seasons which can stretch from spring to fall.
Every year, they know it's coming and
must prepare for a very long haul.**

Most penguins migrate a long way from their homes to the place where they were born. The males arrive first to build a nest. Then call for their partner by honking their horn.

Nearly all female penguins choose the same mate once they arrive. Mama lays one or two eggs, hoping for at least one to survive.

Most penguin parents take turns keeping their egg warm while the other leaves to eat. The egg is kept warm in a brood pouch which is located near their feet.

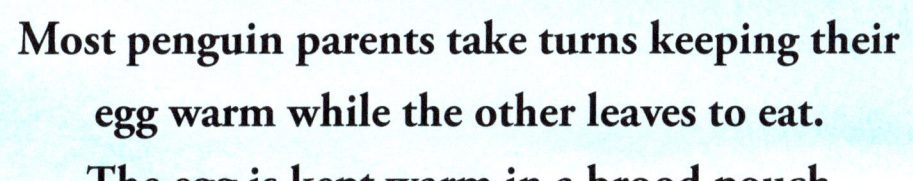

Inside the brood pouch, penguins have an area
of bare skin called a brood patch.
This is where the egg stays warm until it is time for it to hatch.

When they are born penguin chicks look different than their parents, so they can easily be detected. Predators would surely harm them if the chicks were left unprotected.

Emperor

One parent guards the chick while the other goes with a group to find food. They must often swim a long way. The penguins are fuller and slower on their return and must closely watch for foul play.

Soon the chicks have grown enough to be left alone while both parents forage together. While they are waiting, the babies huddle in a crèche. When they return, the parents trumpet their voices and the hungry chicks return to their nest.

Penguin chicks need waterproof feathers before they can swim in the ocean. Soft baby feathers start falling out as juvenile feathers grow in. Parents stop feeding their chicks when the time draws near for them to fledge. When the babies are able to feed themselves, they are left at the water's edge.

Fledgling penguins are in peril the first time they enter the sea.
Unaware of danger, they don't know when to flee.
There is safety in groups, they quickly learn.
When leaving to forage and on the return.

Adult penguins begin molting at the end of breeding season. They start by eating as much as they can to store extra fat for this reason.

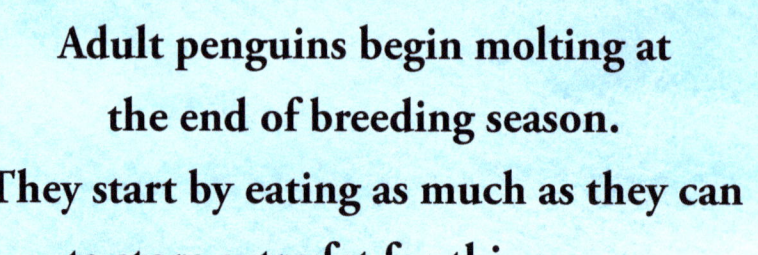

Fiordland

Every feather on their body will fall out, and new ones will grow in before the process is complete. Until all of their feathers have been replaced, they cannot return to the ocean to eat.

The old feathers look straggly and are no longer black.
It takes a few weeks for new feathers to grow back.
Their new coats will keep them warm and dry every day.
Soon they can return to their homes far away.

This is the end of the time penguins spend on land. They can now dive back in the water, proud and grand.

Recognition and Awards

Horses of the Sea
2018 Gold Medal from Florida Authors & Publishers Association

Starfish Gazing
2019 Second Place in the Purple Dragonfly
Children's Book Competition

Sea Turtles Circle
2020 5-Star Readers Favorite Review
Eric Hoffer Book Award Finalist
Purple Dragonfly, Second Place, Age 5 and Up,
Honorable Mention, Age 5 and Under,
International Children's Book Competition Finalist
Readers Favorites Non-Fiction Children's Book Awards Finalist

Coral Gardens

Nonfiction Author's Association Gold Medal

Purple Dragonfly Children's Book Competition: First Place Children's Nonfiction, Second Place Best Illustrations, Honorable Mention: Picture Books Age 6 and Older

Eric Hoffer Grand Prize Finalist, DaVinci Eye Finalist for Cover Design, Honorable Mention: Children's Category

International Book Award Finalist in Children's Picture Book, Hardcover Nonfiction

5-Star Reader's Favorite Review

Dance of the Dolphins

Nonfiction Author's Association Gold Medal Winner

2022 International Book Awards Award Winning Finalist

Purple Dragonfly Children's Book Competition: Honorable Mention Children's Non-Fiction & Picture Books 6 & older

Under the Sea Series

Moonbeam Children's Book Awards Bronze Medal

About the Author

Pat Gleichauf lives in Upstate New York with her husband, Jack. Writing for children is her dream come true. She is dedicated to children's literacy, and her goal is to "hook kids on books." Pat does not miss an opportunity to read her books to students at schools and libraries. She uses this time to encourage children to follow their dreams.

About the Illustrator

Karen Staszko has been creating beautiful watercolor paintings for the past thirty years. She studied watercolor painting for seventeen years and has been teaching it for eleven years. Karen and her husband, Meron, are now living in North Ridgeville, Ohio, to be closer to their daughter and grandson. They lived for eleven years in Southwest Florida. Karen loves art in any form. Her passion is teaching art.

www.ingramcontent.com/pod-product-compliance
Lightning Source LLC
Chambersburg PA
CBHW061157030426
42337CB00002B/29